Second Edition - includes extensive new references and information about the risks of tropical diseases spreading.

Copyright © 2019 Groundhog Press Inc.

I0406264

No part of this document may be reproduced or transmitted in any form or by any means, electronic, mechanical, photocopying, recording, or otherwise, without prior written permission of Groundhog Press Inc. or the authors.

Real Estate	8
New York City - The Big U	12
Why prepare?	14
Temperature variations	18
Diseases	19
Tipping Point - Sudden Changes	25
Worst Case Scenarios	26
How bad will it get?	32
Freaky Weather	35
New Orleans	40
Zoning	42
The Financial Facts of Life	45
Preparing Your Family	56
Drinking Water	57
Food	60
Timeline	62
Appendix I	63

Introduction

Whether you believe the earth is warming because of human action or not, this booklet is still for you. If you do, then it doesn't matter whether you think mankind is wholly or partially responsible. But either way, if you care about the future of your kids and grandkids, then this is for you.

Whatever the cause, whatever you believe you can see:
Summers are getting hotter
Storms are getting worse and more frequent.
Floods are getting worse.
The growing seasons are changing.
Glaciers are melting.
And the sea is rising - records go back for centuries.

This booklet is NOT an argument about what causes climate change.

This is also NOT about whether or how we can combat climate change. It is almost certainly too late to make any useful changes and the climate will continue to change for at least the next 50 to 100 years with consequences stretching into the next millennium.

What this book IS about is how you and your community can plan and prepare for climate change.

One of the biggest changes will come when people realize many coastal properties are about to become worthless. That will destroy family finances but also bring down banks which hold mortgages and the entire real estate business.

This already happened in New Orleans, it is just beginning to happen in parts of Florida and coastal Maryland, but banks are still writing mortgages and insurance companies are writing policies on seaside mansions which climate science says will soon be underwater.

A Union of Concerned Scientists study shows that by the end of this century at least 2,500,000 U.S. properties (homes, schools, churches, businesses, public buildings, roads, airports, and ports) will experience periodic flooding. https://cbsmiami.files.wordpress.com/2019/06/underwater.pdf

Sea level rise is not a theory; it is something that is easily measured.

(Disclaimer: while I am a member of The UCS, I had no part in preparing this report and have no more information about it than what is published for the public to read.)

The only thing I will say about the climate change debate is that, yes, it is true that more than a thousand engineers and scientists have signed on to the position that climate change isn't really going to be as bad as predicted. But the important point is that NONE of them are climate scientists. I wouldn't trust a climate scientist to design a bridge, so why would I believe a civil engineer's opinion about climate change?

The scientists who say climate change isn't happening or isn't going to be a problem all have one of two things in common.
- 1 They aren't climate scientists, and/or
- 2 They are paid by the petroleum industry.

Would you go to a chiropractor for a broken leg? A medical doctor for financial advice?

Climate change is occurring; just look around at the increasing heat in some places and worsening storms almost everywhere. If it isn't flooding, then it is probably a drought.

This year (2019) farmers in the Midwest breadbasket of the United States had to delay planting by two months and if the rains had kept up another two weeks many would have lost their crop insurance and couldn't plant at all.

Next year might be better.

Then again, next year the rain might also last two weeks longer.

Climate change isn't predictable on a small or local scale. Weather is predictable a few days out; climate change is about the average of what will happen over the next decade or century.

In fact, because it is the only worldwide effect, sea level change is the only part of climate change that can be accurately predicted.

Whether you don't believe it is happening at all, or you think it won't be as bad as predicted by most scientists, are you really not going to plan for the possible/likely/certain changes?

Some people refuse to protect their 12-year-old daughters from cancer with a simple, cheap, safe vaccine for HPV because they don't want to believe their little girl will EVER grow up and have sex.

Others refuse to protect their children from measles because one nutty doctor in England once published a ridiculously incorrect article.

But the descendants of those who refuse to prepare for the climate change we already see happening won't be a big political force in the next century - Darwin will take care of that.

Real Estate

I am putting real estate first because, while prices of coastal properties continue to soar, the facts are that billions of dollars worth of real estate is at serious risk of being underwater in just a few decades.

With shoreside properties still going up in price most places, it is obvious that buyers and investors aren't being made aware by the real estate industry of the serious potential for total loss due to the ongoing sea level rise.

People often say that real estate is always a good investment because they aren't making any more land.

Unfortunately, over the next 100-plus years "they" will not only not be making more land there will be less land; i.e., the amount of land above water will decrease every year - therefore SOME property will be a good investment, but not the part along the coast.

People often invest in property that they intend to leave to the next generation and planning for global warming means that you need to think carefully before you invest in real estate.

One particular example of the potential for losing a lot of money in real estate is the state of Florida, which a century ago was known as a place to swindle people by selling them swamp properties.

Later in the last century Florida became a great investment but once more it is becoming a bad deal if you aren't planning on living there for just another decade or so.

In particular, if the most recent estimates of accelerating ocean rise are close to correct, Margarita Land and the rest of the beautiful Florida Keys will be mostly underwater and the massive public works program that connected them to the mainland may become useless because the approach and the sections of highway US 1 that are on the Keys (just another word for islands) will be unusable, either actually under water at high tide or at least weakened by the rising water level.

Don't misunderstand; I loved the Keys when I visited but I wouldn't invest fifty cents on real estate there and you should think twice or ten times before you do.

That is just the most obvious and easy-to-prove example. Many other beachfront and even inland properties will also suffer from periodic flooding (generally defined as 26 or more times each year) or will simply be submerged.

Having a backyard pool can be nice, but when your backyard IS a pool, it's not such a good investment.

Estimates based on existing homes indicate that the total could rise to 2.4 million homes and more than $1 trillion in property damage by the end of the century.

Here are the top 10 cities/regions that the latest study says will soon be mostly underwater:

1. Miami Beach

2. Hoboken, NJ

3. Atlantic City, NJ

4. Key West

5. Galveston, TX

6. Hilton Head Island, SC

7. Lower Keys

8. Mount Pleasant, SC

9. Chesapeake, VA

10. Upper Keys

"Underwater" was first published June 2018 by the Cambridge, Massachusetts-based environmental watchdog group.

"In the coming decades, the consequences of rising seas will strain many coastal real estate markets — abruptly or gradually, but most eventually to the point of collapse — with potential reverberations throughout the national economy. And with the inevitability of ever-higher seas, these are not devaluations from which damaged real estate markets will recover," according to the study."
https://www.ucsusa.org/sites/default/files/attach/2018/06/underwater-analysis-full-report.pdf

So when looking at real estate that you expect to continue to enjoy or to have any value in 30 years, you need to stick to land that is MORE than six feet above the present ocean high tide water level.

And if you want to enjoy a trouble-free property for 50 years you should factor in storm surge from the increasingly powerful hurricanes that can often be another six feet.

That eliminates many of the now popular and expensive vacation properties along the East Coast. Any property that is regularly evacuated if a hurricane is coming will probably be under water all the time in 30 to 50 years.

Choosing property that your grandchildren will enjoy as a beachfront property could be a great investment, although that will be very difficult to evaluate because it won't be close to where the ocean is today.

This is sort of a teaser chapter to get to the most critical information first. There is more on the financial consequences to government, business, and banks in a separate chapter under Zoning.

New York City - The Big U

New York City mayor Bill de Blasio has proposed a $10 billion program to protect Manhattan from rising water levels because even current warming levels will subject nearly 40% of the island to massive periodic flooding within just 30 years.

This is a very ambitious program. Because the important financial district is too crowded and too close to the river/ocean, it is impossible to build a barrier today so his plan calls for extending the southern part of Manhattan by nearly 500 feet with landfill to provide a place to build the barrier.

Unfortunately while the part of the city which includes the oldest skyscrapers such as The Empire State Building is on bedrock, the newer parts of the island are built on landfill and, as with Boston and other cities built on landfill they are both sinking due to the weight of the buildings put up but will also require that any impermeable (water proof) wall would have to extend down to bedrock or the rising sea would just seep under any wall built just on top of the existing ground.

The general plan now includes another sea wall five miles long around Statin Island and gigantic sand berms to protect the Rockaways.

The overall plan will take several years just in the planning stage and part of the problem is where the money will come from. Mayor De Blasio has indicated that the Federal Government will have to take some of the financial burden. Of course with the administration at the end of the decade which fires scientists and demands the removal of even the words "climate change" and "global warming" from agency reports and web sites, it is not likely any such monies will be forthcoming.

This also comes at a time when there are concerns over the power grid after some major outages and when the massive aging city water supply is in need of major repairs. You will understand why when you realize much of the system was completed jst one hundred years ago.

The new tunnel number 3 will cost about $6 billion and consist of sixty miles of tunnel through bedrock.

https://www.dec.ny.gov/docs/water_pdf/nycsystem.pdf

The OneNYC 2050 plan calls for a ban on constructing new inefficient skyscrapers - not banning glass walled buildings, but requiring them to be more efficient to the point of reducing the amount of greenhouse gas emissions from new buildings by 40%.

Something which probably really set off real estate developer President Trump was a proposed requirement to retrofit large existing buildings such as Trump Tower to make them more efficient.

Big U http://www.rebuildbydesign.org/our-work/all-proposals/big-u

Why prepare?

Unless you believe God will never let bad things happen to your family or religious community (conveniently forgetting that the Bible says we are all descendants of Noah's family because everyone else was drowned), it is your duty as a responsible parent and eventual ancestor to take steps to learn about what is going to happen and prepare for it as well as possible.

Remember the parable of the man on the roof of his flooding house.

After all, you don't expect your home to flood or burn down or that someone will hit your car at the next intersection, but sensible people buy homeowners/renters insurance and car insurance even if not required by a mortgage lender or the law.

This booklet is intended to give you the tools to let you think about what may happen as the earth warms overall and how you can prepare your family and yourself, perhaps even your community, for the changes that are almost certainly on the way.

As North Carolina Gov. Roy Cooper said after Hurricane Florence, "When you have two **500-year floods** within two **years** of each other, it's pretty clear it's not a 500-year flood."

This booklet mostly ignores the climate change arguments and instead will focus on the proven changes we can expect as the Earth warms just a few degrees, and how individuals and families can prepare.

You don't need to understand or even believe the reasons the planet is warming or whether humans (that is, politicians) can possibly cooperate quickly enough to stop it in order to see it is happening.

Ninety-eight (98) percent of the hottest days in the last 500 years have occurred this century.

The hottest summers since the US broke free of the Brits have almost all happened in this decade.

On June 28, 2019, France saw the hottest day in the country's history. In 2019, France is reporting the hottest June in history. Last year was the second hottest and killed 7,000 people just because of the heat. Many elderly in French cities don't have air conditioning.

Excessive rains and extreme flooding in America's central region where much of the world's corn and wheat is grown delayed planting by more than a month and some farmers report that they won't be able to plant anything in 2019.

Paradise, a city or 27,000 in California, was wiped off the map by the worst wildfire in California history.

Central Pennsylvania has had 10 times the average number of tornadoes by June 2019. Fortunately, most were the lowest category and caused little damage but almost every following year is predicted to be worse.

In addition to the obvious flooding problems faced by coastal cities, we will face food shortages, shortage of drinking water, the spread of exotic diseases, global unrest, local wars as people fight for food and water, and much more.

The Pentagon ranks climate change as the biggest threat the US military will face in this century, not only because Navy ports will become useless unless completely rebuilt, Army bases will need to be moved or rebuilt, and some Air Force installations will flood, but also because food and water shortages will cause forced migration across borders around the world, causing many local wars.

People will tolerate gangs and drug wars, even oppressive governments, but when their children and elders drop dead due to heat stroke, can't find clean water, and can't get food even if they have money, the flood of people on the southern U.S. border will make this year's expected million look like the line at a Disney World ride.

Food and clean water scarcity are a far more critical concern than other problems and all experiments show that crops will fail more often as the climate generally changes. Rice and corn, which between them feed a large portion of the planet's residents either directly or through meat animals fed grain, are dependent on certain weather conditions.

An unexpected food problem was discovered a decade ago when some people increased the CO_2 level in some greenhouses and also in open fields. As expected, the crops grew more quickly. Unfortunately, it turned out that the fast-growing food crops were less nutritious than their slower-growing cousins.

This can be mitigated by the development of new varieties that can tolerate changing conditions. But these seeds will cost more, making it impossible for subsistence farmers to use them. and, in any case, little work in developing new strains is now being funded and, especially in the US and the Euro Zone, "scientific" farming has reduced the varieties of food crops that are widely planted.

There are many other concerns that worry planners in civil defense as well as the Pentagon planners.

While it is true that as the Midwest breadbasket becomes too hot and alternately too wet or too dry to continue feeding a third of the world, areas further north will become warmer and can be farmed.

Unfortunately, there are already people living on that land who will object violently to being displaced from the land they own and even if they move it takes years to turn a forest or wilderness or shopping center into highly productive farms.

It is simple enough to see if you just think about changing regions of drought, increased drought in some areas, and flooding in others. No matter that other regions will see consistent or even increased rain because the threat comes when millions or even billions of people begin to starve and look for a place to move.

It also matters not a whit whether the increasing temperature is due to human activity or just a natural cyclical occurrence.

Temperature variations

Just as sea level changes are not evenly distributed, temperatures don't go up evenly.

In the U.S. the cities getting hotter the fastest are unfortunately the very ones in the Southwest, which are already very hot.

Las Vegas, El Paso, Tucson, and Phoenix have all gotten a minimum of 4.3°F hotter since 1970 (the year of the first Earth Day).

But nearly every U.S. city has gotten warmer since 1970. and at least ten have gotten 4°F hotter - Philadelphia, Atlanta, and Houston, along with 55 other cities, are 3°F warmer.

A total of six out of about 240 cities in the U.S. have gotten slightly cooler or are unchanged.

Find details about most cities here
https://www.climatecentral.org/news/report-american-warming-us-heats-up-earth-day

Diseases

Something, perhaps the most important thing about climate change which almost never gets any attention is how it will directly affect human health.

This year we are hearing about the disaster barely averted because too many people didn't believe their own doctors and decided their kids didn't need to be protected from measles, a disease which we can easily prevent.

So how bad will it get when we have a lot more people developing diseases for which there is no vaccine even being developed, ones for which it may not even be able to produce a vaccine?

Tropical diseases are already spreading northward due to climate change.

Because global warming changes the habitat and range of insects, especially disease-carrying insects, increased flooding isn't the only danger we will encounter.

Already mosquitoes, lice, fleas, and ticks are spreading into new regions; as winters become milder, their numbers will also increase.

You don't believe that? Perhaps you have failed to notice the vast increase in bedbug complaints in just the past decade. And those little bloodsuckers are just the start.

Dengue Fever, Leishmaniasis, Lyme Disease, and Malaria are just a few of the most obvious serious infections that are spreading to new areas along with the various disease-carrying insects which are responsible.

Dengue Fever and West Nile Virus diseases are unique among those spreading to wider areas in the U.S. because there is no good treatment for either, nor are there any vaccines.

That means you can't protect yourself or your family from either disease with a simple injection even if you aren't a denier and, worse yet, if you catch either you are likely to die.

Expanding habitats will also impact agriculture negatively, further decreasing productivity.

West Nile Virus originated in Uganda but in 2014 killed seven people in New York. This is now the most widespread mosquito-borne viral disease in the U.S.

Dengue Fever is new to this country but is spreading. Usually, people recover with bed rest and, since it is a virus, there is no real treatment. But you do not develop immunity from the infection, so it is not likely there will be a vaccine developed.

Even worse, if the same person gets infected a second time, he or she is at high risk of developing a Dengue Hemorrhagic fever, a very dangerous infection. Hemorrhagic fevers cause internal bleeding and generally act similarly to an acute onset of the genetic condition of hemophilia, making the person vulnerable to bleeding even from minor injuries.

Chikungunya, a gut-wrenchingly painful East African disease (the name in an African language means "bending over in pain") also carried by mosquitoes, recently sickened a dozen people in Florida.

The common deer tick that can carry Lyme Disease is spreading to more extensive areas and are active for more longer periods. Currently, Lyme Disease is the most widely reported viral infection in the U.S (discounting the common cold or flu).

In fact, Lyme Disease has been reported in every state except Hawaii.

An August 2015 study published by the Centers for Disease Control and Prevention shows that Lyme Disease reports have been very under-reported and that over the past two decades the number of high incidence counties in the U.S. went from 69 to more than 260 counties by 2012.
https://wwwnc.cdc.gov/eid/article/21/8/14-1878_article

Over the past four decades, the temperature in the various states has risen an average of 0.3 degrees each decade.

That must seem to a layperson like a tiny and insignificant change, not even noticeable in a room, which is another reason many people have trouble understanding how serious this is.

What people don't understand is that although there will only be a few degrees change on average this century, just as the case with sea levels, there are wide variations with some locations getting much cooler and others warming much more than a few degrees, perhaps up to 10 degrees.

Although Southerners are used to dealing with insects, many in the northern states are not really prepared for an increasing onslaught of mosquitoes and ticks.

Preparation

You can and should adjust your living situation to more extended periods of more intense insect activity.

Window and door screens would be an essential first step.

Personal protection, especially of children, is vital and this may be the end of shorts since the best way to defeat ticks is to wear shoes with socks and long pants with elastic to hold them tight.

Give some thought to your animals, too - not only can they acquire a dangerous infection, they can carry ticks, fleas, or even mosquitoes into your home.

Draining standing water works but may be undesirable - for instance, kiddie wading pools; we kept one filled all summer as a giant bird bath for our six-foot-tall pet emu and grandparents may keep one for kids who visit periodically. There is no need for concern if the kiddie pool is in use every other day or so.

There are very safe and inexpensive biologic materials that, spread on any stagnant water in your area, would greatly reduce the number of mosquitoes because they have a limited range. Dengue Fever mosquito, Aedes aegypti, typically range no more than 400 yards from the pool where they hatched. Old car tires are a significant source of mosquitoes breeding grounds.

Often overlooked in town environments are the storm drain puddles under those drain grates. Even if you have frequent rain, you need to treat these in your neighborhood, perhaps by arrangement with neighbors, since it is an inexpensive material that lasts up to 30 days.

Mosquitos breed quickly but with the increased temperatures the eggs can grow into flying biters very quickly, from first flight to egg-laying in one day, and the next generation takes wing in 10 days or fewer.

This is the preferred control method where it can be applied because the large scale abatement sprays used by cities and towns are toxic.

Even birdbaths can be a place for mosquito larvae to develop, as can fish ponds. Fortunately, the older BTI anti-mosquito bacteria is ONLY deadly to mosquito larvae, not harmful to people, pets, birds, or even fish.

The live bacteria developed by Summit, known as Dunks in the ring version, can be broken or tossed whole on a pond, or you can get an inexpensive chunky version called Bits, which is easy to throw around on any standing water.

Culex mosquitoes is the breed that can carry West Nile Virus and they are most active at night. Unfortunately, they can range more than a mile so, unless your area has mosquito remediation programs, you are out of luck with any local action you can take around your property.

Dengue Fever mosquitoes, on the other hand, feed only in the very early morning and just before dusk, so in an area that has both diseases you are only safe around midday.

A brand-new bacterial repellent extracted from Xenorhabdus budapestensis has been tested and shown effective against Aedes aegypti, Anopheles gambiae, and Culex pipiens mosquitoes which between them carry Zika, West Nile, Malaria, and Chikungunya. It is reportedly more effective at lower doses than DEET.

This is not the mosquito control bacteria produced by Summit Chemical.

There are also some very effective wide-area (about one acre) devices that include a body temperature sticky panel, fan, and even a CO2 emitter to fool mosquitoes into thinking they are live humans. When I had a ranch, we installed four of these and never saw a mosquito near the house or barns. The downside is that you have to keep replacing the sticky pads and the carbon dioxide emitter reasonably often. They also cost in the $200 range but last for years and sure beat making the kids stay indoors all summer.

See the appendix for loads of free reports related to all phases of global warming.

Tipping Point - Sudden Changes

Tipping point is a term you will occasionally hear in the climate change debate and it is important to understand both what that means and what consequences it can have.

A tipping point in this context means that when something gets to a certain point change can go from a gradual evolution to a sudden and very drastic change.

Studies of sea bottom deposits, ice cores, and tree rings have shown that in the past when the climate was changing or even when it was reasonably stable for long periods there were occasional periods when some locations experienced drastic changes in their weather for a decade or more.

By drastic changes they are referencing average temperature changes of from 10 to 15 degrees F. taking place in just a year or two and lasting for several years. An example would be the little ice age that hit Europe and North America from about 1300 through 1870 in two phases, each lasting about 100 years.

This caused severe food shortages because of the shortened growing seasons.

Less than 200 years ago there was a period when the Thames River in London was frozen solid for months at a time and hosted the London Frost Fairs that saw elephants walking across the Thames.

Today and for many years there hasn't even been ice in the Thames.

Worst Case Scenarios

Even though the temperature itself will increase very slowly on average, it may increase a lot in some areas and decrease almost as much in other places so the average increase is small but the local change may be drastic. The same applies to rainfall, drought, and storms.

Is rapid change even possible?

Well, in a word, yes. It is possible. In fact, it has happened many times.

First, we really don't know enough about the climate in general as a process. We can predict weather pretty well, a heck of a lot better than we did in the '50s, although not well enough to justify those silly local weather reports that say one town will be 71 degrees tomorrow while another will be 72. That small difference is easy to measure in a glass of water but almost impossible to accurately measure in a town on a single day, let alone predict.

Those silly TV weather people (even the actual scientists are mere actors and entertainers) on local news shows, just as the presenters are merely teleprompter jockeys reading what other people found out.

Second, there are some major climate features that we know are rather delicate. The well known Atlantic Conveyor is one major climatic feature.

You may not have heard of the Atlantic Conveyor, but you must have heard of the Gulf Stream which is just the surface manifestation of the AC. It stands to reason that if the GS moves warm water north then the water has to get back south somehow and that happens as it cools and sinks, flowing south near the bottom.

The United Kingdom is as far north as Maine and Nebraska but has a climate closer to that of Virginia. It isn't that warm/hot in summer, but England in particular and Ireland generally have very mild winters.

The reason for that is simple; the North Atlantic is a lot warmer than the North Pacific because the warm water in the Caribbean constantly runs north and surrounds the UK, Ireland, and the western part of Europe in warmer ocean water than they would ordinarily have.

What happens is that the very salty waters in the northern part of the Atlantic sink as they cool off. As they sink, they go south along the western Atlantic basin. This warm water rises to the surface and moves north pushed by the inflow of cold water.

But increasing rainfall is causing rivers that flow into the North Atlantic to reduce the saltiness of the ocean, decreasing its density; when this salt water gets "sweet" enough, it will no longer sink when it gets cold which would slow and eventually stop the Gulf Stream.

Measurements show this is already happening.

There could be and probably is a tipping point at some level of salinity where the entire Atlantic Conveyor simply stops. No one knows where that is, but as heavier rainfall in the north increases the flow of fresh water rivers into the North Atlantic (already measured and seen to be occurring now) continues to sweeten the ocean water eventually it will stop. It might take 50 years, or five, no one knows, but we do know it will mean dramatic changes in the weather for the UK and Northern Europe.

This is happening now and will eventually come to a screeching halt. England would then see ice in its harbors, Scotland would see snow like we get in North Dakota or worse because of the ocean that provides the moisture that keeps the UK so wet and green but doesn't feed North Dakota winter snows. France, the Netherlands, and parts of Germany would also see colder winters and cooler summers, reducing their crops and requiring more natural gas or coal or fuel oil to keep warm, further increasing the greenhouse gases pushed into the atmosphere - a positive feedback loop which moves a system away from stability and every new change enhances the next step.

This current is now the weakest it has been since the year 600 AD and has slowed 15 percent since 1950.

The UK is about 25 degrees F. warmer in the winter and 15 degrees F cooler in the summer than Newfoundland. About 20-50 percent of that difference is due to the Gulf Stream. Recent studies showed that wind currents out of the southwest contribute the rest of the difference and they are influenced by, of all things, the Rocky Mountains.

But the winds will also be altered by climate change.

This is one likely tipping point. There are many others.

The history of the climate as easily measured by the air and seeds trapped in ice cores, tree rings, and ocean sediment, show that the climate periodically experiences these tipping points of rapid, almost instantaneous changes in the climate.

Instantaneous in terms of the Earth and climate change can be a few decades, or even a few years.

The bad news is that there is virtually nothing you, me, or the government can do to deal with very rapid climate changes - millions, more likely hundreds of millions, would die and there is very little anyone can do - that is why experimenting with the Earth's climate by pumping lots of greenhouse gases into the air is a very high stakes game even if it really isn't the cause of climate change.

It is one of those situations where the outcome if experts are wrong and there is no climate change, the negative consequences of trying (improving efficiency, reducing pollution, and saving money) will be mild. The benefit of not changing is also relatively small too, we are saved the effort and expense involved in working to make life better,

However, if experts are correct and climate change is not only coming but its effects will be drastic, we could face the end of our current civilization. Therefore we should all be working to slow or prevent climate change but politically that seems impossible.

The end of civilization isn't as far-fetched as you might think.

Studying DNA from millions of people, it has been found that about a million years ago climate changes reduced the human population to between about 15,000 and 25,000 on the entire Earth.

Again, about 150,000 years ago (called Marine Isotope Stage 6 because of how it was discovered) we had a major cool-down and the number of humans dropped to less than 1,000 TOTAL everywhere. In fact the number was thought to be as low as 600 survivors from whom everyone today is descended. DNA surveys can easily show how few ancestors the present population actually had.

Hunter gathers could survive major changes in the climate when they lived in small numbers, but a technological civilization would probably become extinct.

Again about 70,000 years ago, Sumatra essentially exploded in a gigantic volcano (similar in size to what would happen if the gigantic Yellowstone and Campi calderas blew simultaneously. (Campi underlies Mount Vesuvius and a surrounding wide area including Naples, Pompeii and Herculaneum.) That global freeze caused by volcanic ash whittled down the population to between 1,000 and 10,000.

Do you think that no one would want to live near those potential massive volcanoes if they really were a threat? Well Vesuvius erupts all the time and we know it blows its top periodically but people still live in Naples.

People stayed on the slopes of Mt. St. Helens even when they were told it was about to erupt, and they died.

So, yes even when science proves that something is dangerous people won't even relocate to save their lives so simply saying no one is preparing for climate change doesn't mean it isn't happening.

The point is that the human race has come close to extinction many times and nature doesn't notice or care.

How bad will it get?

Part of the problem for laypersons trying to understand the competing claims are the seemingly endless changes in scientific predictions.

What the deniers say is that this means the scientists aren't in agreement about the fact of global warming when the true position of climate scientists has always been that the planet is, on average, warming.

The only disagreements are about how fast it is happening but even the early conservative scientific consensus was that a 1.5°C increase in global temperature would take place in this century.

That 1.5°C would cause a sea level rise of two to three feet by the end of the century.

Unfortunately, all subsequent studies based on measured increases in global temperature are all higher and by 2010 the conservative estimates had risen to a likely 2°C rise, not in 80 years but in 30 years, exposing 570 cities housing 800 million people to regular damage from storm surges.

Many government officials in coastal cities have failed to tell their residents and businesses that they are in danger and have not even begun to make appropriate preparations for the inevitable.

"The World Economic Forum's Global Risk Report 2019 shows, around 90% of all coastal areas will be affected to varying degrees. Some cities will experience sea-level rises as high as 30% above the global mean."

This is because the ocean level at various places is going to vary considerably due to the undersea terrain, currents, and prevailing winds.

Unfortunately for the U.S., the worst unequal water level rise is occurring along the Eastern and Southern coasts.

Some cities, such as New York, are fortunately built on bedrock, but many others, like the downtown business district of Boston, are built on top of a landfill.

Other cities are on solid ground but not bedrock and in both instances, the enormous weight of millions of people, skyscrapers, streets, buildings, and even cars is actually causing many of the largest coastal cities to sink, which only amplifies the threat of rising sea levels.

Adding to the population pressure, which will cause more wars and global economic disruption, some cities are sinking very quickly.

Some areas of Jakarta, Indonesia - population 9.6 million - the ground has sunk 2.5 meters in nine years. At the same time, the local sea level has risen by an average of three feet each of the last three decades.

Many Asian cities will be badly affected because they are built on land not much above sea level, to begin with and even have large populations living on boats (probably the least endangered) except that the oceans are rapidly being fished out with ever-decreasing catches.

But while you may be thinking that what happens in Asia doesn't mean anything to you, I hasten to remind you that most of today's electronics, and even solar panels, are manufactured in those cities.

Current estimates say 80 percent of people in the world will be directly affected by sea level rise in just 30 years and that is based on the current estimates - recall that every new estimate has placed the warming and sea level rise higher than the last.

Already nearly 100 coastal cities in the U.S. have chronic flooding. In 20 years that number will double.

No amount of effort to curb burning hydrocarbons or trees, or planting new trees, can have any positive effect in 20 years.

The majority of European cities will be affected.

Around the world, the numbers of displaced people and closed businesses will begin to have a serious economic and human impact within just a couple of decades, even in the most advanced countries.

Even completely landbound countries such as Switzerland will experience changes in weather patterns and growing seasons, which will change even that country.

Freaky Weather

As an example of extreme weather events I was going to write about the recent terrible flooding in Houston and the Mississippi and Missouri basins here but a much more dramatic example just occurred.

As I was writing this section on July 1, 2019, news from Mexico came across the wires. At the start of summer the city government in Guadalajara, Mexico, was dealing with five FEET of hail.

This was so preposterous that many thought it was a hoax, but it really wasn't, Mexico in the summer was actually having the worst winter weather in history. An ice storm that we have never seen in northern Maine hit a region where the average temperature for July 1 is around 90 degrees.

Since this is a booklet about preparing for climate change, the question is how do you prepare for this sort of extreme weather.

In short, you can't.

Some things you simply can't prepare for other than to buy or build a very strong, well-built home.

Miami is a good example of a more gradual threat that the city and county are working to mitigate but in 2012 New York experienced another of the freak tipping point incidents.

New York City (possibly even city resident Donald Trump) got a shock in 2012 when Hurricane Sandy (only a Category 1 storm by that time) caused a storm surge high enough to pour seawater into the electric-powered subway system in lower Manhattan.

But while that took a direct hit from the remnants of a superstorm that had piled up water along the northeast coast for days, other East Coast US cities are experiencing extreme weather events every year.

Miami is ground zero for climate change flooding in the US, as is the entire state of Florida, but other cities are already experiencing it to a lesser degree and it is getting worse.

Some Miami neighborhoods are now flooding even when there is no major rain event, sometimes when there has been no rain for days.

Sea level rise is not very big yet but, because of the porous limestone underlying much of Florida, water can rise up from the ground with the slightest change in sea levels because that increases the pressure on the groundwater.

Norfolk, VA, and especially its gigantic US Naval Base are experiencing periodic floods as well, but only (ONLY!) during storms or heavy rains. The base is in an area that is as flat as a crepe and, even worse, much of the installation is built on landfill. Periodic flooding causes the landfill to settle a bit, and a bit is all it takes to increase the number of flood events.

Norfolk and other East Coast cities are also experiencing problems with floods during storms but the situation in Miami is much worse because all it takes to flood expensive high rise condo basements with their BMWs, Porsches, and Mercedes is a full moon.

Sea levels rise not only because glaciers and ice shelves at the poles and places such as Greenland are seen to be melting but also because of something most people simply don't understand.

When water warms up it expands. Not much, but a lot of the Earth is covered by water, often very deep water and hence a very large volume of water, so even a tiny percentage expansion can make big changes.

Water is densest at its smallest volume, just above freezing. Fortunately for all life on Earth, ice is less dense than liquid water. If ice weren't less dense than cold water then as ponds, lakes, and even oceans froze in the winter the ice would sink and build up each winter until most of the Earth would be covered in ice with just a small layer of liquid water on top.

That is obvious but most people don't really think about that or realize that as water warms it continues to expand; from near freezing to 95 degrees it expands a couple of percent.

The sea levels in Miami are predicted to rise between three and five feet by the end of this century. What we are experiencing today is the result of just the predicted rise of a few inches since the 1990s.

But it turns out that even the terrible consequences of a one-foot rise in sea level predicted from the '90s to 2030 is very conservative.

Since 1992, Miami sea levels have risen 3.5 inches and that has been enough to cause periodic flooding in parts of the city.

The unfortunate fact is that back in the '90s it was predicted that sea levels would rise by 12 inches by 2030 but now it is realized it will actually be much worse.

This is one of the problems with the science deniers. They point out the fact that earlier predictions were off and neglect saying that while the scientists were wrong, they were too conservative - already, climate change effects are worse than predicted, not better, and the latest predictions are much worse.

The most recent projections as of early 2019 is that instead of temperatures rising four degrees F by 2100, they will rise by more than nine degrees. Remember that the 2.5 degree increase you kept hearing about were in Centigrade so the latest projections aren't that out of line. But that amount of temperature change means sea levels would rise by more than six feet in the next 80 years.

If the latest predictions are accurate (remember every subsequent revision to climate change threats has shown that it will be WORSE, not better). All East Coast cities will become unlivable, displacing (at today's population level) 200 million people in the US.

That six-foot rise in sea levels would also submerge about 700,000 square miles of the US; that's about three times the present size of California.

While that is the worst case scenario of the latest study and is given about a five percent chance of occurring, according to the people who created the study, it is again important to recall that EVERY new study shows things are worse than earlier predicted and even a sea level rise less than six feet will be disastrous.

Imagine standing at the edge of the ocean at high tide. If you are five foot six inches tall, your nose would be at water level later this century.

In 2017 Miami voters approved a $400M bond issue, half of which would be used to mitigate sea level rise.

> If the predictions are even close to being accurate every penny spent to protect the Miami area from the consequences of climate change are totally wasted so while it looks as if this was a good mitigation effort by the city of Miami, it is a boondoggle. The money should be spent building a NEW Miami further inland, although most of Florida will be submerged in another 150 years so further thought should be given to what constitutes useful mitigation.

New Orleans

Fun City South (aka The Big Easy, The Crescent City, or The Big Crescent), New Orleans, has demonstrated the weakness of plans to wall off coastal cities from the ocean's encroachment.

The disastrous events surrounding massive hurricane Katrina, which left nearly 2,000 dead, probably won't be repeated because people know the danger now.

However, in July 2019 a mere heavy rainstorm piled up water on top of the Mississippi, which was already eight feet above its usual level after the terrible spring rains and floods.

So New Orleans was again flooded, with Bourbon Street underwater on the tenth and eleventh, just from six inches of rain falling over a one day period.

But the city was also threatened by Tropical Storm Barry, which promised another two feet or more of rain over a two-day period as it very slowly made its way northward.

In addition, there are likely to be 70 mph onshore winds that could cause a storm surge running up the river, causing a 15-foot rise in the river level, overtopping many sections of the levees protecting New Orleans.

To a dispassionate observer, seeing streets filled with several feet of water from just six inches of rain and knowing a gigantic water-laden storm was coming along in just two more days would suggest abandoning the city now, let alone not spending hundreds of millions of tax dollars that would all be wasted in just a few more years.

Yet real estate prices in the better areas of New Orleans were still creeping slowly higher, so educated, literate, and financially stable people able to get a mortgage were making the largest investment of their lives in a region that was virtually guaranteed to be underwater in a few decades.

So New Orleans teaches us two lessons. First, despite being given nearly unlimited amounts of money, no coastal city can really hold back Mother Nature even without a major storm striking. Second, we see a prime example of how vast populations can simply ignore the physical and economic facts of life.

The more important lesson is probably the latter - when people look around at their prosperous neighborhoods and hear the politicians calmly saying how this is not global warming they will be lulled into sticking it out, trusting the lies of both those politicians who deny global warming is happening and the other politicians who see the water rising but fight to keep their positions by refusing to admit they simply can't adequately prepare their cities.

Fortunately this time New Orleans dodged a bullet because Barry dropped most of its water load elsewhere but it was a very close thing and many other coastal towns were flooded.

Zoning

People are all in favor of zoning laws when they stop a junkyard being started next door to their suburban home but they get quite upset when they want to build or especially rebuild a home in a location that will almost certainly be flooded in the next big storm or hurricane.

It gets worse when people are told they can't build or rebuild because the ocean is rising and in 20 years the plot of land will be under a foot of seawater off and on (mostly on), but the water is rising and whether it continues at the present slow rate or jumps a 2 feet overnight when half of Greenland and the McMurdo Ice Shelf both slide into the ocean at the same time, it won't matter to you or your home's foundation which cause destroyed it.

Restrictive zoning with an eye to future water availability and levels is a major, simple, and very obvious step government and ONLY the government can take to mitigate future problems.

For example, many people in the middle of the country this year have lost their homes and may never recover financially since their biggest investment is now gone and, since they weren't in the 100- or even 500-year flood zone they weren't required to purchase flood insurance and most didn't. It might not even have been available if they had wanted to buy it. The fact that 500-year floods are now happening in many places once or twice a decade is worth factoring into your plans.

In fact, many of the homes near the big rivers in the heart of the US are almost new because they were built on the foundations of the homes that were flooded a few years ago.

A lot of the vacation homes along the East Coast are also nearly new for similar reasons.

Restrictive zoning laws seem to homeowners like government overreach at its worst but while rebuilding 100 or 1,000 homes every year in five-year flood zones (which were 100-year flood zones a decade ago) is a waste of resources we can easily absorb; when 10,000 homes and businesses are destroyed every year at the same time when we need to rebuild roads, bridges, sewers, and water supplies, even the resources of the US will become stretched.

Historical records show that sudden climate changes can occur causing temperature swings of 15 degrees F up or down. In New England a winter that averages 15 degrees instead of 30 would be inconvenient and would stretch resources but wouldn't be a disaster.

However, the recent high temperature in Atlanta, GA, was 103 degrees. What if instead, it was 118 degrees? Power lines would stretch and transformers would fail so even air-conditioned homes and offices would be Sahara Desert hot in July - only humid, not dry - and wouldn't rapidly cool at night as a desert does.

People would drop like flies, so too would flies but that wouldn't be any comfort.

This is actually happening every summer in France and they don't even burn coal for electric power.

In 2017 it was 115 degrees for 36 days in Las Vegas. Add 15 degrees to that and at 130 degrees day after day AC systems will become overloaded and begin to fail. I saw this happen decades ago at a TV station in Boston where heat and humidity were overloading the AC system I was responsible for and that was just a typical Boston summer combined with an extra load on the studio lights.

Winter temperatures 15 degrees colder in much of the southern US would mean frozen water and sewer lines along with people freezing to death in houses that don't have northern type heating systems or the gas lines or oil supply infrastructure.

That should give you a clue as to some of the things we can do to prepare for climate change.

Tornados will be stronger and more frequent, as will hurricanes. Houses need better insulation plus enhanced heating and cooling systems, and cities need to prepare their water and sewer systems not only for the problems of climate change but also to handle the increased population as people's homes flood and they move to cities and towns inland.

When some cities flood, for example New York City, millions will be moving. That will be a slow-moving disaster so there won't be riots and a mad rush to evacuate but it will occur pretty quickly in the scheme of things.

People in Tornado Alley need to go back to the pioneer building method of digging up sod and piling it to make a house half underground. Only, of course, going underground using modern building techniques, cement and insulation instead of sod. That would moderate heat and cold as well as getting away from tornados.

The Financial Facts of Life

While human life and safety is the most important consideration, cities and nations live and die by their finances so a major real estate crash would greatly weaken any country, even the mighty US.

Cities and towns rely in large part on real estate taxes to provide city services. In addition water, sewer, and sometimes trash collection charges help keep towns alive financially.

So, what happens when those sources of money dry up as people and businesses leave and the tax base shrinks?

It so happens that we have a horrible example right here in Detroit. When the auto industry collapsed the city went from the wealthiest in the country to the poorest in little more than a decade.

By 2000 many parts of Detroit didn't even qualify as slums. They are more properly classified as ghost towns.

A friend of mine in high school had a son who studied automotive engineering and design. He did great at GM. But today, unless he continued his education in other areas of engineering, for all I know he may be asking if you want fries with that.

Now consider if real estate collapsed in value not just in one large city, but a dozen large cities and thousands of small towns all within a decade or two?

Current average estimates of sea level rise and the Zillow estimate of current property values, by 2045 (little more than 25 years now), suggest that we as a country will lose $136 billion dollars in real estate value.

That's just the value of periodically flooded and therefore nearly worthless properties. Then consider the businesses even tourist businesses, banks, groceries, fast food places, boat rentals, and so much more, all of which will collapse as the most expensive properties drop off the tax rolls and the towns can't continue to support fire, police, road maintenance, sewer, water, and other services.

That is the result of about 300,000 flooded properties by mid-century; continue on another 50 years and by the end of the 21st century nearly 2.5 million residential and commercial properties will be worthless, as will be the local banks that financed the town and the mortgages.

In today's dollars, and by then inflation would have normally doubled or tripled the values; that is more than $1,000,000,000 in real estate losses.

Now factor in the increased spending needed to build more homes for those people and finance the infrastructure to support those additional eight million people.

In Miami-Dade County where this is already taking place there is, according to local papers, only a slight drop in real estate valuation.

Bankers and real estate developers who won't be there in 20 years are understandably not interested in spreading this risk information - not even those who do see what is happening. As for the politicians they support, political concerns are always local and always focused on the next election, why would they campaign on the coming collapse of their town?

I leave building contractors out of the blame game because, after all, they are like plumbers, electricians, and other trades people who are simply making a living by filling orders.

But just because the politicians are short-sighted doesn't mean YOU and your family and your business need follow them down the rat hole.

And those politicians, emergency management coordinators, and city planners who do see the coming problem face the fact that there are no easy solutions, sometimes no solution at all.

Consider that the Miami area is investing billions on reinforcing sea walls, breakwaters, raising critical infrastructure, and more, but that is all based on the average expected threat. All of that money may be completely wasted because every subsequent estimate of future seal level rise is higher than the last. By the time those remediation steps are completed they may already be outdated.

Or, perhaps not, but it is certainly possible and it is certain that eventually they will be underwater.

The following numbers and estimates are taken from a large study made by the Union of Concerned Scientists, which provides many references you can follow up if you desire.

The economic effects of rising sea level predictions that have already proven accurate except when they underestimated the actual rise, which has been as much as double the earlier estimates, so, while imperfect, those estimates form a minimum base from which to determine the costs.

The oceans are expected to rise a minimum of five feet, possibly as much as 10 feet by 2100, that is in the lifetime of many children.

The average estimate places the rise at 6.5 feet and that is used as the foundation for the calculations of actual property values - there is no guesswork involved in this.

The study, "Underwater" found that even within my projected lifetime (I retired a number of years ago), that is, within 12 to 13 years (the study was published in June of 2018 and the estimates were made over the previous year.) about 150,000 homes and 7,000 commercial buildings with a current value of $63 billion, will be flooded on an average of twice each month.

That will displace 280,000 people, more if the coast continues to be developed.

By the end of a 30-year mortgage, 2045, those numbers will double, destroying the value of the land, homes, businesses, and government infrastructure.

Although the results of climate change are already obvious in Dade County and the Miami area in particular, the damage won't be limited to Miami and Mar a Lago but will include 120 communities along all US coasts, or 20 percent of the current tax base.

Thirty of those towns and cities will lose half their real estate tax income, which means cuts to schools, emergency services, and much more.

Many of these properties won't actually be under water, but they will flood so often that they will be worthless except as beaches.

While many of these areas, especially on the southern and eastern coasts, are used to short term disruptions due to hurricanes, they are notably unprepared for permanent alterations to their coastline.

Both Florida and, perhaps surprisingly, New Jersey, will be the hardest hit at least at first, with both losing about 60,000 residences by 2045, within the lifetime of people just retiring to a seaside home.

Ocean City, NJ, alone has more than 7,000 homes at risk.

But while NY, NJ, FL, and CA all face losses in excess of $1 billion, no coastal state escapes scot-free. Louisiana might be thought to be at the greatest risk since New Orleans is already below sea level but it will be comparatively unaffected simply because so much has already been destroyed and much of the at-risk coastal property is already low-priced.

Although the UCS estimates that extreme action to reduce carbon dioxide emissions could reduce the number of at-risk properties 80 percent by 2060, as a former Washington journalist with decades of experience and simply an aware citizen, I don't see any possibility that the US will make that sort of drastic change.

DENIERS

A note about climate deniers is appropriate in any book touching on climate change and while some are not reasonable, others have a very good basis for their belief and some scientific data to back it up.

There is more than one kind of denier.

Many people self identify as climate change deniers; that is, they don't believe most scientists, but they fall into several very different groups.

So, a brief look at what different kinds of denial really mean.
1. It isn't happening - global warming total deniers. Anyone can see the extremes of weather are increasing and any gardener knows growing seasons are getting longer on average with the USDA climate zones moving north so much that just the past 50 years have seen garden plant growth zones in the US moving at least 100 miles further north. And, if that isn't your personal experience, scientists have been measuring temperatures very accurately for many years There is ZERO evidence for this reasoning, but there are some very reasonable and potentially correct reasons to deny some parts of climate change.
2. Humans aren't the cause. Although there is a vast amount of evidence that increased pollution caused by burning fossil fuels and increased methane release from natural gas drilling and even cattle has gone exactly in step with an overall warming trend, this is an understandable criticism of the CAUSE of climate change, but not the reality of it.There are various

reasons why people might want to think that human activity isn't responsible for a change in the climate. People don't like change and preventing the worst of climate change consequences would require drastic changes in how we live. Even the many countries that did sign the Kyoto and Paris protocols aren't taking any serious economy endangering steps to combat climate change. China, for example plans to start up one large coal-fired power plants every two weeks for the next decade.

3. The final and potentially the most reasonable denial is the group who admit that climate change is happening (many say it is anthropogenic) but believe it won't be as bad as the experts predict, i.e. better than average estimates This may be true. It might also be worse than the average estimates say. The question remains whether it is prudent to make long-term plans for the average or even the more extreme potential predicted changes - especially since the predictions keep getting worse as more data are collected.

After all, if you are hit and killed by a car, does it really matter who was driving and whether it was an old Volvo or a new Ford and that the accident was due to a bad brake job?

You are still dead.

In the same way, it really doesn't matter whether you believe a particular theory of climate change; extreme weather is getting worse as anyone can see for themselves - there is less clean water to drink, pollution is increasing most places, and sea levels are rising.

That last is simple; there are tide gauges that have been used for a century and they show water levels are rising - there is no theory involved. One in San Francisco first got wet in 1854.

Right up front you should understand that as a retired emergency management coordinator of 30 years (not to mention being a trained scientist and science writer) I always look at the worst case scenario that, in climate change, keeps getting worse with every newly published study and simulation.

That is actually the job of those who work in emergency management, planning for the worst and hoping for the best. But it would be useless to provide anything less than the worse case plans when you are concerned with preparation for protection of lives and property. You can always do less when the time comes.

And, while some people point to the fact that estimates of sea level rise and other problems keep changing, what they fail to tell people is that those estimates invariably get WORSE, not better.

In other words, yes, climate scientists aren't certain how bad it will get, but every time they see new evidence they don't say it won't be as bad as they previously said; it will be worse.

Some estimates and studies show sea levels will rise not just a foot by the end of the century, but six to 12 feet based on the latest data.

One very influential scientist agrees with those who think it won't be as bad or as difficult to cope with as most climate scientists say.

His name is Freeman Dyson and if you look him up on Wikipedia you will find he is highly respected as a theoretical physicist who has put forward some very interesting if controversial ideas that have featured in many science fiction books and movies. But please note that he is NOT a climate scientist and by his own admission quickly gets bored with subjects and never goes into any great depth.

So while Mr. (not Dr.) Dyson is entertaining and has had many provocative ideas, he doesn't deny climate change is happening; he just disagrees with the estimates made by climate scientists who run thousands of hours of simulations on supercomputers. The best you can say for his position is that his is a gut feeling that since humanity has survived so far we will find a way to cope this time too.

However, it wouldn't be proper to write about climate change without looking at some of the theories pushed by the fossil fuel industry. Remember, for 50 years cigarettes were sold on TV and just two decades ago tobacco executives all swore under oath before Congress that nicotine isn't addictive.

The global coal, oil, and natural gas business is worth an estimated $4 to $6 TRILLION dollars per year. Their bias is easy to understand.

Climate scientists get paid the same whether they find there is no climate change or that there will be a major even disastrous changes.

According to studies published by the National Academies of Science and Technology (food security), climate-induced shocks in grain production are a major contributor to global market volatility, which creates uncertainty for cereal farmers and agribusiness and reduces food access for poor consumers when production falls and prices spike.

One study, by combining empirical models of corn production with future warming scenarios, shows that in a warmer climate, corn yields will decrease and become more variable. Because just a few countries dominate global corn production and trade, simultaneous production shocks in these countries can have tremendous impacts on global markets. The same study shows that simultaneous shocks will become much more likely as the climate continues to warm. That study emphasizes the need for continued investments in producing more heat tolerant grains.

There will be roughly 10 billion people by the middle of this century so, while climate change will put increasing pressure on food production, at the same time demand for food will be increasing.

Feeding the world will be increasingly challenging as the climate grows warmer. Some studies also indicate that after a growing region reaches the best temperature for growing corn (which seems to be the climate in the Great Plains a decade ago) further increases will reduce yields no matter how much fertilizer is applied.

A number of studies are available at http://www.pnas.org/keyword/food-security.

The consensus is that if the temperature in the four major corn-producing countries (87 percent of world production) increases by about six degrees F then production yields will begin to drop just when the population is increasing. In fact, the chance of a 10 percent decrease in corn production is 86 percent in a given year.

This will cause a price increase in this cheapest of all food and there are already about 800 million living in extreme poverty.

Crop projections can be downloaded from
https://mtigchelaar.github.io/maize-variability/

Price volatility numbers are available at
http://www.pnas.org/keyword/price-volatility

Find additional supporting information at
www.pnas.org/lookup/suppl/doi:10.1073/pnas.1718031115/-/DCSupplemental

Preparing Your Family

How to prepare for climate change depends first of all on whether the change will be gradual or sudden.

The rise in temperature will certainly be gradual, so gradual that, like the proverbial frog that sits in a pan of water as it is heated not noticing the slow change until it is cooked. Preparing for a gradual change in the climate will pose many problems, such as what happens when the sea rise pushes people out of their coastal homes - yes, they can move, but WHERE? Any place a couple million people want to move as their homes become increasingly unlivable will turn out to have people already living there.

Even worse, those settled people are probably already stretching the capacity of the infrastructure to its limits so adding a lot more people will mean lack of water, more crowded roads, and stresses sewage systems.

Given enough time building new homes is easy; we do it all the time.

We can also build new reservoirs and reduce the amount of water we waste if we can do so gradually.

The same goes, although not as easily, with agriculture. Already people don't like to live next to cattle feedlots, and farmland is constantly being paved over for parking lots serving ever newer shopping centers.

Amazon and delivery by Walmart and other chains will eventually reduce the demand for new physical stores, but reconverting already destroyed farmland will be a major task.

So much for gradual changes, but what about the unexpectedly sudden climate change? The sort of thing which can happen if the climate reaches a tipping point.

Power lines should be buried (they should have been a century ago); cell towers should be reinforced and more should be built to keep people in communication and make certain they have internet.

A small solar power panel costing a hundred dollars or less will power a laptop computer.

In a decade you will be able to power an entire household with economical solar panels because the prices are dropping almost monthly.

Drinking Water

A major problem facing even families in technologically advanced places will be finding safe drinking water.

Whether your location has too much rain or too little, there will be less safe drinking water.

If too much rain plagues your region, then sewage treatment plants will be literally swamped and wells will periodically be underwater, leaving rivers and ponds as major sources of drinking water.

Distilling water is simple technology but did you ever consider how much energy it takes to boil a gallon of dirty water?

Solar stills are cheap and simple; just get a container to hold the water, paint the bottom black, place it in the sun and water will start to evaporate. Add a cheap plastic sheet and something to collect the water that drips from it; just a pan in the bottom middle of the tank will do but you can fancy it up with a siphon.

Cheap, and simple enough for a child to operate.

Unfortunately that solar still will only produce 0.3 liters of water per hour for a square meter tank.

A family of four will need about 12 liters (three liters per person per day) or a five-square-meter tank if you have a full day's sunlight, more in winter and much more if it is cloudy.

A large tank is impractical and a lot of small ones take up a lot of room and constant work to maintain.

But scientists have just discovered an inexpensive gel made of commonly available chemicals that, by weakening water bonds, can greatly increase the amount of water that evaporates.

The increase in efficiency by taking less heat to vaporize water is about 12 times more efficient than the best commercial solar still today.

This gel would make a solar still producing about 3.6 liters of water per hour for a one-square-meter tank. That means just a one-square-meter tank (so small it is easily portable) would produce enough clean water for a small family.

In the short term, a cloth filter and a gallon of ordinary bleach will get you through a few days of clean water shortage.
A teaspoon of household bleach (don't ever buy the kind that includes soap) will sanitize a gallon of water without boiling (if you don't have running water you probably don't have electricity either).

Ten drops will do for a half gallon.

Use double if in real doubt; just wait for the bleach to break down, which can take a day or more.

Yes, you'll be drinking a chemical, but that's just city water anyway although they often use chlorine gas.

https://is.gd/9h24No

Making certain local officials and your descendants know about this technology could save lives.

Buying one or two of these chemical gels when they are available is a good investment. In mid-2019 a million or more people in the central US could really use access to clean drinking water because all the wells are under river water, as are many of the buildings.

Getting these new solar stills to areas that are already short of drinking water could greatly ease the pressure to migrate to better regions and potentially avoid a lot of small wars, any one of which could blow up into another global war.

Food

While it is simple enough to prepare to turn even ocean water into potable water, food is a very different matter.

This is, unfortunately, a very, very short section because, while it is possible for preppers and members of the LDS church to stockpile a year of food (living in a rural area we always stock a two-week supply of food in my home, even more in a bad winter), no one can stock up with 30 or 40 years of food.

The best you can do is make certain your home is someplace where you can grow your own food and that means living on several acres of land at a minimum with your own water supply.

There simply isn't enough room for all of today's city dwellers to move to the country, especially since the amount of land will be shrinking.

But food will continue to be produced and distributed in the more advanced countries so everyone who is reading this booklet really only has to pay attention to changing conditions and be ready to adapt to the changes as they occur.

However, there are bound to be disruptions in the food supply even in the US, so don't be like those people who strip the shelves of grocery stores when a storm is due; follow FEMA suggestions to have a week's supply of food on hand at all times. It isn't difficult or expensive for most people; just keep using the oldest supplies and replacing them with fresh.

Since canned goods last for several years and both rice and dry beans last for years if you keep them dry, perhaps in Mason jars; your diet might be boring but you certainly won't starve if roads are closed for a few days as they often are in Northeast winters.

Merely knowing what is about to happen can be a big advantage since most people won't have any idea.

There is no particular item you need to stock up on because there won't be any particular major shortages. Large factories, unless they are overseas and thus vulnerable, are seldom next to the ocean.

As I said, this is a very short section but is also perhaps the most positive one because a bit of common sense will get you through.

Timeline

Drastic changes to the environment where you live may take decades, but with the potential for a tipping point or one of the statistically likely events such as a meteor strike or a giant volcanic eruption, there is a good possibility that the world could face a significant climatic event somewhere on the planet, perhaps in many places.

Of course a meteor strike in a really bad place, such as one of the gigantic calderas, could change the whole picture and bring the race to the brink of extinction in months and that's all she wrote, but since there is no amount of planning that can save your family from that kind of global disaster we can simply ignore them.

If you want to understand how fragile civilization really is, you can pick up a copy of my book
"Saving the World from Asteroids and Planning for Coronal Mass Ejection threats" for only 99 cents (Amazon sets mandatory minimum prices or it would be free).

https://www.amazon.com/Asteroids-Planning-Coronal-Ejection-threats-ebook/dp/B00M2I68HC/ref=asap_bc?ie=UTF8

But the focus of this booklet has been how to prepare your family and your community for the rapidly approaching changes in the earth's climate.

Appendix I

The National Academy reports may require you to open a free account but while the print versions of the very detailed reports are expensive, there is always a free download of the same document.

- Environmental Engineering for the 21st Century Addressing Grand Challenges (2019)
  https://www.nap.edu/catalog/25121/environmental-engineering-for-the-21st-century-addressing-grand-challenges

- Modeling the Health Risks of Climate Change

- Workshop Summary (2015)
  https://www.nap.edu/catalog/21705/modeling-the-health-risks-of-climate-change-workshop-summary

- Exploring Lessons Learned from a Century of Outbreaks Readiness for 2030: Proceedings of a Workshop (2019)
  https://www.nap.edu/catalog/25391/exploring-lessons-learned-from-a-century-of-outbreaks-readiness-for

- Framing the Challenge of Urban Flooding in the United States (2019)
  https://www.nap.edu/catalog/25381/framing-the-challenge-of-urban-flooding-in-the-united-states

- Protecting the Health and Well-Being of Communities in a Changing Climate Proceedings of a Workshop (2018) https://www.nap.edu/catalog/24846/protecting-the-health-and-well-being-of-communities-in-a-changing-climate

- Responding to the Threat of Sea Level Rise Proceedings of a Forum (2017) https://www.nap.edu/catalog/24847/responding-to-the-threat-of-sea-level-rise-proceedings-of

- National Academy of Engineering 2017. Responding to the Threat of Sea Level Rise: Proceedings of a Forum. Washington, DC: The National Academies Press. https://doi.org/10.17226/24847.

- https://www.ucsusa.org/sites/default/files/attach/2018/06/underwater-analysis-full-report.pdf
- Disaggregating sorghum yield reductions under warming scenarios exposes narrow genetic diversity in US breeding programs http://www.pnas.org/content/114/35/9296?utm_source=TrendMD&utm_medium=cpc&utm_campaign=Proc_Natl_Acad_Sci_U_S_A_TrendMD_0
-
- Jesse Tack et al., Proc Natl Acad Sci U S A Temperature increase reduces global yields of major crops in four independent estimates http://www.pnas.org/content/114/35/9326.long?utm

_source=TrendMD&utm_medium=cpc&utm_campaign=Proc_Natl_Acad_Sci_U_S_A_TrendMD_0

- Tao Li et al., Proc Natl Acad Sci U S A Economic aspects of global warming in a post-Copenhagen environment.
http://www.pnas.org/cgi/pmidlookup?view=long&pmid=20547856&utm_source=TrendMD&utm_medium=cpc&utm_campaign=Proc_Natl_Acad_Sci_U_S_A_TrendMD_0

- William D Nordhaus, Proc Natl Acad Sci U S A Rice yields decline with higher night temperature from global warming
http://www.pnas.org/content/101/27/9971?utm_source=TrendMD&utm_medium=cpc&utm_campaign=Proc_Natl_Acad_Sci_U_S_A_TrendMD_0

- Shaobing Peng et al., Proc Natl Acad Sci U S A Auxins reverse plant male sterility caused by high temperatures
http://www.pnas.org/content/107/19/8569?utm_source=TrendMD&utm_medium=cpc&utm_campaign=Proc_Natl_Acad_Sci_U_S_A_TrendMD_0

- Tadashi Sakata et al., Proc Natl Acad Sci U S A Increasing probability of mortality during Indian heat waves
http://advances.sciencemag.org/content/3/6/e1700066.full?utm_source=TrendMD&utm_medium=cpc&utm_campaign=TrendMD_1

- Elisa Ragno et al., Sci Adv Climate models predict increasing temperature variability in poor countries
http://advances.sciencemag.org/content/4/5/eaar5809?utm_source=TrendMD&utm_medium=cpc&utm_campaign=TrendMD_1

- Sebastian Bathiany et al., Sci Adv Crop yields expected to fall as temperatures rise
http://science.sciencemag.org/content/357/6355/1012.6?utm_source=TrendMD&utm_medium=cpc&utm_campaign=TrendMD_1

- Emily Morris, Science Heritability for Yield and Glycoalkaloid Content in Potato Breeding under Warm Environments
https://www.degruyter.com/view/j/opag.2017.2.issue-1/opag-2017-0059/opag-2017-0059.xml?format=INT&utm_source=trendmd&utm_medium=cpc&utm_campaign=trendmdOA

- Manuel A. Gastelo Benavides et al., Open Agriculture Productivity of a doubled haploid winter wheat population under heat stress
https://www.degruyter.com/view/j/biol.2012.7.issue-6/s11535-012-0097-1/s11535-012-0097-1.xml?format=INT&utm_source=trendmd&utm_medium=cpc&utm_campaign=trendmdOA

- Krisztina Balla et al., Open Life Sciences
https://www.degruyter.com/view/j/biol.2012.7.issue-6/s11535-012-0097-1/s11535-012-0097-

1.xml?format=INT&utm_source=trendmd&utm_medium=cpc&utm_campaign=trendmdOA

www.ingramcontent.com/pod-product-compliance
Lightning Source LLC
Chambersburg PA
CBHW030018190526
45157CB00016B/3124